USING PEOPLE

HOW TO GET AHEAD IN WORK & LIFE

AILEEN BENNETT

featuring photos by
Gwen Aucoin
(and others)

Coyright ©2010 Aileen Bennett

All rights reserved. Printed in the United States of America. No part of this book may be reproduced in any manner whatsoever without written permission except in the case of brief quotations embodied in critical articles and reviews. (Please send us copies of these for our enjoyment). For information, contact Two & 21 (bookinfo@twoaand21.com)

Cover photo by Gwen Aucoin (gwenaucoin.com).

Other photo credits at back of book.

ISBN: 978-0-9832462-0-6

10 9 8 7 6 5 4 3

This is a book about people.

This is a book about business.

This is a book about how they are the same thing.

CONTENTS

Sometimes it's good to see things from a different angle

Page	Title
8	Whatever business you are in....
10	Talk about people **behind their backs**
14	**Always** judge a book by its cover
18	Become a **nun**
22	**Act** like a **3 year old**
24	It's all about **making a connection**
28	We can see through **your disguise**
32	It's all about **you**
34	**You** are a **magnet**
36	You've been **framed**
38	Put on your **crazy glasses**
40	**Lie** to yourself
42	**Give up** on your dreams
46	Be all **ears**
48	**Flip** a coin
50	Sweat the **small stuff**
52	Your children aren't **listening**
54	You are talking to **yourself**

56	Start **small**
58	Which box…
60	Notice **everything**
64	Know **your** mind
66	**Steal** shoes
68	**Never** forget a name
72	Your strength is your **weakness**
74	**Beautiful** on the inside?
76	How you treat the waiter
78	We all need a **wingman**
82	I need a **break**
88	Run with **scissors**
90	**Ask**
92	**Respect** your competition
96	What if life **is** a dress rehearsal
98	Stare at **models**
100	**A cup of** coffee
105	This page is a **gift**

Whatever business you're in...

YOU'RE IN THE PEOPLE BUSINESS

Sometimes we get caught up in reports and lists and sales figures. They are not your business. People are.

It's people that buy your product or services. In a world full of resources, people are your most important resource.

When it comes down to it (whatever 'it' is), we do business with people we like and trust. We may justify our decisions on price, quality, delivery times, locality and all sorts of things but, given any kind of choice we do business with those with whom we have good relationships.

If you want to be successful in any business, you have to be in the people business.

Let's all start Using People. Now.

TALK ABOUT PEOPLE BEHIND THEIR BACKS

Yes, go on - you do it anyway. We all do. It's part of being human.

It's all very well for me to get all virtuous and say you shouldn't, but I think it's impossible not to. People are fascinated by people, by what they say, what they do, what they wear, by who they are seeing and by how much they are earning. If you are going to become a master of using people you are definitely going to have to admit you talk about people behind their backs.

I call it networking.

As the American journalist, Edgar Watson Howe said:
"What people say behind your back is your standing in the community."

What you say behind people's backs is a direct reflection of who you are. I try, (I don't always succeed, but I try), to only say things behind someone's back that I would say to their faces, or something better. I love to tell on people, to share how good they are at something, or what a great service they provide. Making them look good makes me look good. If you are the one who suggests someone who provides a great service then a little speckle of that kudos reflects on you.

Tell people good things about others. Share the thoughtful things they do, the little things they notice, the times they go out of their way for a stranger. Recommend other business people. Tell your boss about a co-worker. Point out something that would otherwise go unnoticed. Don't share the bad stuff, there are enough people doing that already and you don't want that associated with you in any way. Share the good stuff. It will make you stand out.

Imagine a world where no-one ever talked about anyone without them being there. Social Media would grind to a halt, nothing would go 'viral'. PR companies would no longer exist and all our brand building efforts would be completely wasted. Clients would have trouble finding you and we'd never know about half the new restaurants in town.

If you are in business, you want your customers and clients talking behind your back. It's essential. Facebook, Twitter and other social media mean that we now have ways to directly praise or condemn a company publicly. Many commerce sites allow and encourage user comments and reviews.

It takes some courage to welcome true feedback - the good and the bad. I know, personally, that I will read customer reviews on commerce sites before I read the 'marketing speak' if indeed I ever actually read the marketing speak. I am not put off by a few bad reviews, in fact, I'm slightly concerned if they are not there. Motivational speakers like me have been spouting off about transparency for years. It comes at a price.

I write a communication column for my local paper, I often end up writing about customer service. I have a rule that I only name the companies that I am praising. Anyone else doesn't deserve the publicity. Unfortunately most of your customers don't think this way.

On a personal level, what you say about people tells others a lot about you. If you spend your time 'bitching' or being negative you will get a reputation for thinking that way, however justified your complaint is. If you spread gossip about someone I will presume you will also spread gossip about me.

We all need to vent sometimes. To say some stuff out loud just to get rid of it. To complain about something that is just 'not fair'. Have one or two people that understand this and will not judge or remember what you say. Venting is like a trip to Las Vegas, what happens there stays there. It is never referred to again or bought up as 'evidence' at a later date. We cannot control what others say about us. Only what we say about them.

You can always console yourself with Oscar Wilde: "There is only one thing worse than being talked about, and that is not being talked about."

When you catch yourself saying or thinking bad stuff (and we all have those moments) ask yourself - Why? What about that person or situation makes you feel insecure? What are you hoping to achieve? Is it really about them or are you trying to make yourself look bigger or better?

I won't always be the right speaker for every job, but I can still help my clients by recommending someone who is a good fit for that particular event. If I help them find someone good it makes me look good. It gives me better connections with others in my industry who may, in return, suggest me to their clients or collaborate with me on some fun future project. It also cements my relationship with my client. If there is a loop, I want to be in it.

ALWAYS JUDGE A BOOK BY ITS COVER

I remember my mother telling me at an early age "don't judge a book by its cover" - it was a popular thing to tell your children back then, and apparently still is. Sorry Mum, I disagree. We judge on appearances. However nice it is to think that we don't, we do. I even would go so far as to say we should always judge a book by its cover.

I was a graphic designer for many years and a lot of work goes into designing book covers. In a bookstore hundreds of books compete for your attention. The average consumer looks at a front cover for about four seconds before turning over to the back cover and reading for maybe seven more seconds. When sales reps show up at bookstores they usually only have the covers with them - talk about judging a book by its cover!

You are reading this book - I wonder if the cover helped?

Did you get dressed randomly in the dark this morning? Do you just go to your nearest clothes store and buy whatever they have in your size and budget? For most of us the answer is no. We take time over our wardrobe decisions, we dress in a certain way that we think reflects who we are, or the job we do, or who we want to be seen as. Even those people who swear that what they wear isn't important to them are making a statement with their appearance.

We are a visual society, we have

come to learn to judge things very quickly based on visual appearance. Watch a two or three year old in a store, they instinctively already know which products are aimed at them and which aren't. They have already learned to judge visually.

Of course I know what my mother really meant when she handed down her sage advice. She meant that sometimes appearances can be deceptive, that you shouldn't judge anything purely on how it appears. That once you've read the book you will have a much more valid opinion than if you just look at the cover. Of course, the same applies with people. Once you get to know them your first impression changes. Still, it doesn't mean that we shouldn't take that first impression into consideration, simply because it's the impression they have chosen to make.

The story of singer Susan Boyle had the world captivated. When she auditioned for Britain's Got Talent, the video of her performance went viral, breaking world records for the number of views on YouTube. We watched as people judged her on her appearance and then were wowed by her vocal ability. Would this have been so great a story without that first judgement? Without us knowing she was a spinster living with her cat, some of the impact would have been lost. The story became a global sensation because of our judgement. Susan Boyle portrayed herself exactly as she was and that is what tugged at hearts across the world. We loved that, in so many ways, we got exactly what we saw. A simple woman with a rare talent.

We have so many ways to show ourselves to the world today, our clothes, our facebook/twitter profiles, our websites, our blogs. They are all 'covers' and we should be aware that sometimes that's all people know of us. What we choose to present to the world says a lot about who we are. Let's make sure it's saying the right thing.

You'll find out as

you read this book that I'm all about you 'being you' - your authentic self, as people have taken to calling it. If everything that you put out there into the world (business and personal) reflects who you are, then you can't do any more than that.

You cannot control the judgements that people make, they are operating from their own belief system and experiences.

Judge a book by its cover but still read the book. It may have hidden greatness.

BECOME A NUN

OR AT LEAST...
GET A NEW HABIT

(pause for you to groan at the bad pun)

Every time I show this slide to my audiences, I ask them how long it takes to create a new habit. The answers don't usually vary much - most people tell me between 21 and 30 days. They have heard this, they have read this, and they have tried unsuccessfully to create habits so therefore, it must be true.

I then ask how many of them have ever smoked. Hands go up:
 "How long did it take you to create that habit?"
The answers don't vary much. One day, one cigarette, one puff.

Isn't it strange how we are convinced that good habits take much longer to adopt than bad ones.

I think that with the right motivation and the right consequences any habit can be formed instantly. We have to know that the new habit gives us more pleasure than the existing one.

The first habit to break is to stop believing what you read in books (including this one). Think about what you have read and see if it applies to you and your life. If it doesn't, please feel free to never think of it again.

Yes you have permission. Act like a 3-year old, and do it often.

As we get older, sometimes we forget what we knew instinctively when we were younger.

As we get more 'grown up' we have these things called agendas, calendars and to-do lists. Sometimes we live by them instead of in the moment.

Imagine this:

You are taking your 3-year old to the park, you know you can walk there in ten minutes, spend 20 minutes in the park and then walk back. You have scheduled the time. Right on time you set out of the door. Your 3-year old doesn't realize that the fun is meant to start when you get to the park and starts having fun straight away, looking at stones or leaves they find on the walk there. You grab their hand and tell them to hurry so you can get to the park and play and start having fun.

They are already playing. They are already having fun. Sometimes it's not about your plans, sometimes it's about the moments.

How much of your life are you missing because you never live in the now? Are you waiting to celebrate at the end of the big project, or waiting to relax when the next quarter is over? Are you always telling yourself you'll be successful after the next promotion or that you'll start looking after your health once the next report is out of the way?

The problem with that, is one thing is replaced by another and we never celebrate, relax, feel successful or make time for ourselves.

There is only one time to be happy, one moment you can enjoy. It's right here, right now.

Ask any 3-year old. They know.

IT'S ALL ABOUT
MAKING A CONNECTION

Some people say business is about who you know - your connections. It's really about who you connect with. You may have lots of connections without much connection.

Be real, be genuine, BE YOU. When you are being you, you give others permission to be themselves and that can only be a good thing.

If you are a con-man (or woman) or someone that only sees each customer once and never has contact with them, or anyone that knows them, ever again, then you can disregard this advice. If, however, you want to build business relationships, gain trust and client loyalty, you may want to start making a connection.

I live in the South where people are famous for being friendly. They hug, even in business. We all know instantly whether a hug is real. Whether the person giving the hug means it or is being fake. A fake hug, like a fake handshake or a fake smile, does more harm than good. We all know the person doesn't mean it. That there is no real connection.

Whatever your version of the 'fake hug' is, whether you say "We must do lunch sometime" or "I'll call you", please, let's stop it now. It doesn't work, we don't believe it. If you don't have something genuine to say then don't say anything.

If you don't like or trust me, don't do business with me. We will both be much better off.

There are people who judge the success of a networking event by how many business cards they gave out or received. If you don't remember the people you met, there was very little point in going. If they don't remember you, you wasted your time. If you just want a list of businesses in your area use the phone book or an online directory.

This isn't about numbers, it's about people. People can achieve amazing things when they work together, and making a connection is

the first step towards that.

When you are given a chance to talk about what you do, don't just spout of some rehearsed information. Connect. To quote Maya Angelou: "I've learned that people will forget what you said, people will forget what you did, but people will never forget how you made them feel."

With all the ways we have to connect today, it should be easier than ever. Sometimes it seems like there are too many ways of staying in touch but too few where we make real connections. It's surprising the impact a phone call, or an in-person visit can have these days.

Remember that what ever business you are in, you are in the people business.

Attend networking events, not just those that interest you, but those that interest your client base. I make a point of attending conferences that are outside my areas of expertise. I learn new stuff that I can apply to my business but most of all I meet new people that I wouldn't have come into contact with had I stayed in my own field.

Be genuine. Be real. Make a connection.

Sometimes we all try to hide who we really are. We may hold ourselves back in certain situations because we are trying to find a way to fit in. We may lack confidence and try to make ourselves feel better by acting differently. We may feel we have to prove that we are smart, or cool, or hardworking, to gain the respect of those around us. Whenever we act from these positions we are not truly being ourselves and people can tell.

I have seen people put others down to make themselves look better. I know I've even done it myself at times. It doesn't work. It makes you look bad, it makes them feel bad, it makes them feel bad about you.

Whenever we disguise ourselves people can tell. Pretending to be someone else just doesn't work.

The world would be very simple if people could just see your insecurity and know that's what it was, but that's just not what happens. Others can usually sense that something is 'wrong'. They don't know what the wrong is. They can tell you weren't being genuine or open but have no idea why. They make up their own reasons.

In business this leads to a lack of trust. Your customer doesn't know WHY you are not connecting with them, they just know you aren't. They attribute it to a lack of confidence in your service or product.

Acting as though you are more confident, more outgoing, more knowledgeable, more anything, is dangerous. It can come across as fake. We all have been advised at sometime to 'fake it till you make it' and I remember myself using that philosophy. Now I would tell someone to be confident in what you do know, and strive everyday to know more. Natural confidence, (knowing you know), is addictive and attractive to others. People who really know their stuff, and themselves don't have to make others feel 'less than' to make themselves feel 'more'.

If your work doesn't allow you to be yourself, or doesn't encourage the personality traits you possess, then it's not for you in the long run. If you have to be deceptive about who you are, it's time to leave. Look at the things you are good at, the things you do naturally - find a job that works with these strengths. You will be much happier and much more successful.

Seek out the people who are being themselves, they will always be open and share what they know. They operate from a world of abundance that comes from being secure in themselves.

So drop the disguise, we can all see through it.

BE YOU.

IT'S ALL ABOUT **YOU**

You always suspected it was didn't you?

Read on.

YOU ARE A MAGNET

By now you have all heard about 'The Law of Attraction' - it's one of those things that everyone's talking about. There are books everywhere telling you how to get what you want.

You already know how. You are already getting everything back that you put out there.

The Law of Attraction is just what happens all of the time. I'm not particularly 'touchy-feely' but I do know that I get back what I give. I love quantum physics and the theory that everything is connected. I believe that thoughts are things and are more powerful than most of us ever consider.

Like attracts like. It's amazing how many negative people you can attract just by muttering "it's not fair" and how many positive people you see when your outlook is bright.

It's about noticing the right things. The things that help you in your life.

YOU'VE BEEN FRAMED

We often judge situations by the context we place them in. The frame we put around them.

We remember past experiences and use them, rightly or wrongly, to judge our present circumstances.

If, for instance, every time you were called to 'the office' at school it was because you were in trouble, you are likely to worry slightly when you hear your boss wants to see you. If you only met with the school Principal to get praised and informed of the latest awards you had won, you probably have a different feeling.

We frame each experience and label it so it is there to recall when we need it. We must always remember that we created these frames and they have a limited view. We may remember a childhood incident of our father demanding perfection as a negative thing while it would be quite possible to reframe the experience as a loving action.

Frames are neither good or bad - they just are. We use them whether we are conscious of it or not. Let's be aware when we prejudge a situation. Sometimes just being aware can change our thinking.

You may think books with pictures in them are for kids. It may be time to change that frame.

PUT ON YOUR CRAZY GLASSES

Every day we get to choose how we see the world. We often let outside or unconscious influences dictate this for us.

We sometimes let the weather decide our mood before we even get out of bed. Or we announce that, because there was too much traffic or the wait was too long at the coffee shop, we are having a bad day.

Some days we should all wear crazy glasses. I'm talking metaphorically here, but you can take me literally if you like. It would certainly change the way you perceive the world.

We have to get aware that we control our perspective on the world. Wearing crazy glasses changes that perspective. Look for the unusual, or the comical, or the absurd but most of all look for the creative, the artistic, and the little guy who's doing things differently. They are everywhere, they just choose a different view of the world. There is an abundance of evidence that you can make a living doing what you love. That you can follow your own instincts, by not following the herd.

Of course you can use your crazy glasses to see anything you want. You get to choose, as always.

LIE TO YOURSELF

You already do.

We always think we know what other people are thinking. We make assumptions as to what they are thinking and then we act as if those assumptions are true.

We all do it, a lot. We do it with complete strangers, we do it with our customers, our co-workers and our bosses.

Once we believe something, we then, subconsciously, collect evidence to prove ourselves right.

I'm not asking anyone to stop presuming things. It's how we are wired. I'm suggesting (very gently and in an English accent) that you acknowledge that they are just guesses as to what others are thinking and not the truth.

In fact, our assumptions say more about us than they do other people (read that again).

Our assumptions reflect our own thoughts back to us. If we feel insecure in certain things, we are likely to assume that others think we are not good enough either.

If you are going to keep lying to yourself (and you are) then at least, make it a good lie. Tell yourself good stuff. Pretend that complete strangers are thinking positive things about you.

You are making it up anyway.

GIVE UP ON YOUR DREAMS

(yes, I mean it)

MAKE THEM INTO **GOALS**

Make a list of all your dreams and cross off those that no longer excite you. Sometimes we think we want something and we don't really. I used to think I wanted to live on a yacht, when I really just want to go sailing occasionally. Question yourself - What things do you really want to happen? What do you really want to achieve? Imagine each thing coming true and see how you feel about it.

If they don't completely match who you are, let them go. If they are too small, give up on them, and do it with a smile. You have bigger fish to fry (that's just an expression - this hasn't turned into a cook book).

Hopefully you will have some things on your list that you just refuse to give up on. Things that you know are meant to happen. Stuff you instinctively know you should be doing.

Keep those. They are YOUR dreams, not societies, not your parents. The things that you have a sneaking suspicion that you were born for. Now you need to take steps to make them happen. Get uncomfortable, get planning.

Now you can dream.

Write your goals down. In detail. Every little thing you can imagine. Enjoy daydreaming about them. Dream with a purpose, on purpose.

Dreaming should become an everyday thing. Visualize exactly what you want. Enjoy it as if you already have it. Use the internet to help you plan. Use your imagination. Use anything you want.

You will probably find it impossible not to take the next step if you have followed the instructions so far. Take action. Start doing little things (or big things) each day to get you nearer to what you want, or what you want to be.

You were given your dreams for a reason. **Act on them**.

BE ALL EARS

Most of us don't listen enough. While we are 'listening' to someone we are often simply forming our next sentence in our heads and waiting for a chance to interrupt.

I have researched advice about learning to listen and I have to say most of it was pretty bad. Lots of pointless stuff like 'pay closer attention' and 'don't let your mind wander' but no instruction on how to do these things.

Listening is an active thing. We already know how to do it. If I were to offer you a million dollars or the secret to life to listen to every word I said for the next five minutes, I bet you could.

My advice would be:

Be genuinely interested in the other person. Ask questions if you don't understand or want to know more (and if you care you will want to know more). Make sure you understand both the other person's point and point of view.

Realize that it's listening, rather than talking, that makes you an expert and a leader. You learn so much more when you really listen.

I believe that you don't only listen with your ears but with every sense you have. It takes them all to really grasp what someone means.

This may seem strange advice, coming from someone who makes their living as a speaker, but it's precisely because of what I do that I understand the value of listening. After all it's really my living.

If you are the one speaking, whether one to one, or on a platform in front of thousands, you need to make your words easy to listen to. You are equally responsible for what the other person hears.

Your choice of words, and the value you place on them, your tone and intonation, your pace and volume and your connection to the listener all have a big part to play.

I believe that 'the meaning of communication is the response you get'* so if someone doesn't listen to you, you need to change your communication.

So it's all down to you, the listening, the talking and all the communication in between. After all you can't change anyone else.

*thanks to Richard Bandler for the definition

BIG DECISION? **FLIP** A COIN!

Yes, you read that correctly. When you have a decision to make (big or small) flip a coin.

Take notice of your reaction to the result. If you find yourself immediately saying "best of three" or your heart sinks at the result, you have your answer. Go with that feeling rather than the result of the flip.

This is simple and effective and works, for me, every time.

If you want to know what you really want to do, go ahead, flip that quarter. It's worth a try.

SWEAT THE SMALL STUFF

I know someone wrote a book telling you not to do this, but, as I've said before, you should ignore what you read in books and make up your own mind.

**Sweat the small stuff.
The small stuff is the important stuff.
The small stuff is the big stuff.**

Whether the economy is thriving or really scary, it is the small stuff that matters: the people and the memories. The things you look back on and smile. The moments, the shared experiences.

You know what I mean. I don't want to sound like an insurance company commercial here. It's not soppy or silly, it's just what's important.

OUR CHILDREN AREN'T LISTENING

(They are more intelligent than that)

It's what you suspected all along - your children aren't listening.

I'm not saying they don't hear what you say, they do (even when they are pretending they don't). They just don't take much notice.

They are more clever than that. They are watching what you do. That's how they really learn.

If you are telling them to live their dreams and follow their hearts, but you are not doing the same, they soon get the message that 'grown ups' settle for things.

If you lecture them regularly about having a positive attitude and you complain all the time, they are learning from you.

They will follow what you do, not what you say you do.

Think about it, we all did the same. If we had listened to our parents we would have been very different, probably very boring, adults who never took risks and saved half their allowance for their retirement from the age of 10.

Imagine if at thirteen years old you knew what you know now. Would life look the same?

Your children know they have to live their own adventure. Or at least I hope they do. They are going to watch you for signs of how to do that. Show them, don't just tell them. Make sure your life is a good example of all the things that you wish for your children.

This doesn't mean you have to stop lecturing them, talking to them and passing down your wisdom. In fact it's essential because...

YOU ARE ALWAYS TALKING TO YOURSELF

When you give advice, listen carefully. You are always talking to yourself.

START SMALL - THINGS GROW ON THEIR OWN

This book nearly didn't get written. I'd been planning it for a while and then when it came down to actually writing, I was overwhelmed.

What would I wear on Oprah? Did I need to lose weight to look good enough? How would I celebrate its first week on the New York Times Best Seller list? What would people expect from me next? Would my friends think I'd changed?

I laughed at myself (eventually) and realized this was just the current book. There will be more. It doesn't have to be perfect, it just has to be done. If it is a huge success and I end up on the sofa with Oprah.. well I guess I'll just worry about what to wear when that happens.

Sometimes we all get caught up in worrying about the future - stuff that hasn't happened yet. It's quite possibly the worst way to waste time ever.
Start small. Let things grow on their own.

The puppy in the picture?

Yes she grew. Big enough to destroy a sofa all by herself.

WHICH BOX ARE YOU **THINKING OUTSIDE** OF?

In the last few years we have all been thinking 'out of the box'.

I have news for all of you:

There is no box.

If there was a box there would be plenty of ideas left inside it because we have all spent so long thinking outside it. If you do have a box to think outside of, please send it to me, I'd love to have all those ideas that no one else wants.

Ideas are not good or bad, they work for you or they don't.

As long as you are thinking and being creative, you just don't need a box.

NOTICE **EVERYTHING**

If people are our only real resource then we need to know a whole lot more about them.

Most people tell us everything we need to know, if we would only learn to notice.

Just having a conversation with someone will show you who they are. The more we notice, the more we learn. The more we learn, the more we can connect.

There is nothing more flattering that someone paying attention, wanting to know about you. Not in a 'creepy, stalker, ask a lot of personal questions' type of way, more in a 'you matter to me, your opinions matter to me' way.

If you can work out how people process information, you have an easy way to begin a connection. People tend to take in their environment in one of three ways: visually, auditorily, or kinesthetically. In other words we use images, sound and feelings.

Most people have a preferential method, or a combination of methods that is natural to them.

With a little practise and study you can learn to notice this very quickly and that gives you a huge headstart on connection.

We all use different senses in different situations, so when I say 'a visual person', I really mean someone who is being visual in that moment. Some individuals have a very strong leaning towards one sense, others switch depending on their mood.

Visual People are all about pictures (no shock there). Their eyes move up to find the answer to a question. These are the people in an audience who 'look like they are listening'. Their breath tends to be quite high and shallow, they sound excited easily. They will often use their hands to show you their pictures. The hands are held quite high.

They use visual terminology "I can't **see** that happening", or "Let's **focus** on this"

Listen to the words they use. When they are telling you that 'something is all a blur' they literally mean that they can't make a clear picture of it. They need their picture to be clear so that they can process it. Help them. Talk about focus, clarity, brightness, color, viewpoint, new perspectives, sketching things out, reading between the lines, anything visual.

Auditory people take in information via sound. They breathe from the middle of their diaphragm and their voices often have a nice flow or timbre and expression. If you ask a question they will likely look to the side, toward their ears before they answer. Auditory people will say things like 'that rings a bell, or that sounds good'. Words about sounds. Sometimes you will notice them turning their heads slightly. They are paying attention by turning their ear toward you. Most auditory people use their hands to express thoughts but hold them in quite a small area directly in front of their body.

Kinesthetic people are governed by feelings. Feelings are physical (touch) and emotional. They tend to sit low in a chair and look down before they answer a question. They breathe from low in their diaphragm and as a result have lower voices, and answer more slowly than other 'types'. After all they have to check their feelings about a subject and that takes longer than looking at a picture. Their vocabulary relies on words that involve touch or feelings. "I can't quite grasp that idea," "We are on solid ground," "This feels right," "We hit this one out of the park".

Identifying these types is not meant to put people in boxes (you know how I feel about boxes). It's meant to give you some clues into how to notice and what to notice. Many people are combinations of types. On a productive day someone may be both visual and auditory, but when they are having a rough day they may be all kinesthetic. Being able to notice this is amazingly valuable. Wouldn't it be great to be able to guide that person back to being productive with just a conversation.

You may have clients that respond well to sports analogies or food comparisons. People tend to show you who they are, we just need to notice.

It's amazing the information that people will tell you if you know how to look.

KNOW YOUR **MIND**

If you are going to find out how other people think, you should definitely spend some time working out how you think.

How you think is who you are. Find out how you work, find out about your brain. It's probably the only one you will ever have.

Find out what helps you listen, how you get interested in things. Look at what you remember easily and what you don't. Find out why.

We all make good decisions and not so great ones. If we can work out what we did differently in the decision making process then we can make more good decisions.

Think of buying clothes. You've all bought clothes, right? Some things you've worn again and again, and other items have languished unloved in the depths of your closet for years. Why? What was different about the buying process? Which senses did you use? Did you worry about what they looked like, or their texture, or the logic of what they would go with? Did you feel more relaxed on one day, or more stressed during a last minute purchase? Did you like the color or the fit or just the way it made you feel?

I always know when I'm going to wear something I purchase by the way I stand when I put it on. It's not very deep but it's how I know.

We all have things that we are naturally good at, and things we remember instantly. Some people remember dates, others people, others just strange facts about baseball. Find out how you do these things. I don't have the answer, only you do.

Be your own mentor. Study yourself. It should be interesting.

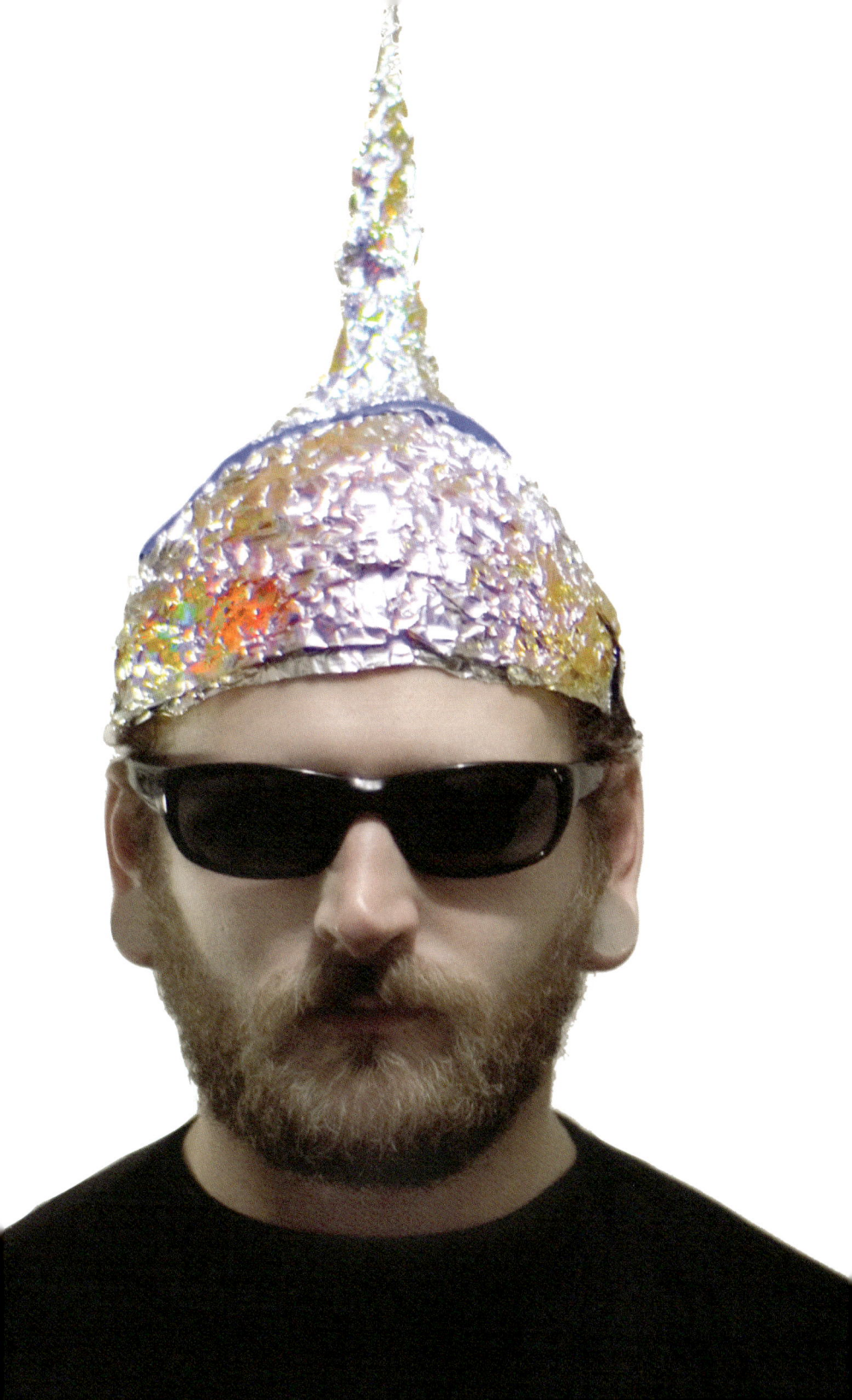

STEAL SHOES

and then send them to..
No not really, as much as I love shoes. Don't steal shoes. Don't even try on others people shoes but do imagine what it's like to walk in them.

We all think our service, or our product is the best and that people will rejoice when they find it and that it will be the solution to at least one of their problems. We can't even hope to do that unless we walk in their shoes (figuratively). We have to know our customers needs and wants and day to day problems before we can be of any help to them.

You may have an employee or colleague who is consistently late or seemingly lazy. If you want to keep them (and keeping them costs much less than replacing them) you may have to find out the reason behind their actions. Get to know them and their challenges, you may be surprised. An employee who is understood and helped to be better is often the most loyal worker you will have. Does your company understand the needs of employees that have families, or passionate hobbies, or love to do volunteer work? If you can find out what is important to those workers, you will be able to understand their needs so much better, be able to make rewards tailored to the individual and have a happy, efficient workplace.

Is their some little service that you can offer your customers that would make their life just a little easier? It's a great way to say thank you while building brand loyalty and an understanding of your client base.

Put yourself in someone else's shoes.

NEVER FORGET A NAME

How many of you consistently forget the names of people that you meet?

I'm sure some of you have read books about how to improve your memory. I did. I tried to attach each name to a silly object but only ever remembered the object, never the name.

Then I realized that I remembered some names. Hmmmm. I believe (as you may know by now) that if you can do something once, and figure out how you did it, you can do it again. I wasn't bad at remembering ALL names. I found two things that immediately helped me:

1. I found that if I actually heard the name in the first place I had a much better chance of remembering it. So often we are too busy thinking about what we are going to say that we forget to listen to the other person. We then try and recall a name that we never heard in the first place. Not an easy feat.

2. I faced the truth. You are not going to like it. We remember the names of those we think are important enough*.
Ouch.

Think about it. If you have just met someone who you think may be your next boss, wife, sugar daddy, or best friend you are not likely to forget their name. You don't have to think of a letter and make it rhyme with an animal and make a picture just to remember. You don't even think about it. You put it in the place in your brain where you keep the names you need to remember.

So I now make sure I listen to the name, and make that person important enough to remember.

*Obviously if I meet you, and then don't remember your name then I'm just bad at remembering. You are very important to me.

There is another side to remembering names, a side that is often neglected. Helping people to remember your name.
Make it easy on them.

1. Pronounce it clearly, even on the phone. I can't tell you how many companies I call and they mutter some kind of auditory shorthand into the phone. I have to ask if its "insert company name' and then I get that sigh 'yes' as if to say "I just said that, didn't you hear me" Not a great start.

2. Associate your name with something if possible. Mention the place you met the person before or someone you have in common.

3. Introduce yourself with your name the first few times you meet someone. It's better for them to say "of course, I know you" than let them be embarrassed because they have forgotten.

4. Make yourself important enough to remember.

YOUR STRENGTH IS **YOUR WEAKNESS**

YOUR WEAKNESS IS **YOUR STRENGTH**

It's amazing how often we find that our strengths and our weaknesses are the same thing.

I ask audiences to list the strengths of an elephant (size, weight, maybe a great memory etc.) and then ask them to list the weaknesses, the two lists are often identical.

It is the same with people. Your lack of formal education may be a weakness, but it is also your strength. Your ability to think differently, your enthusiasm, your need to understand details, your lack of social awareness, your control freak ways. All of these can be qualities that work for you, or against you.

When I first started speaking I was told that my regional accent would prevent me from being successful. I didn't sound posh enough. Now, living in the USA, having an English accent is an asset. It's always best to stick to being yourself.

Embrace your strengths, and your weaknesses. They are all you.

WE CAN'T TELL IF YOU ARE **BEAUTIFUL** ON THE INSIDE UNLESS YOU **SHOW IT ON THE OUTSIDE**

I keep hearing people say it doesn't matter what you look like on the outside as long as you are beautiful on the inside. Really?

We all look much the same on the inside, scientific marvels yes, but beautiful? Not in the traditional sense of the word.

I think beauty comes from confidence and happiness and how you treat people. I would love to see what they look like on the inside but I can't. I can only see what you show me on the outside. Your actions. Your attitude.

I will make assumptions based on those. I will also make assumptions based on how you present yourself to the world (go back and read Always Judge a Book by its Cover)

I don't care if you have the latest haircut, or if you have tattoos. I don't care if you use botox or not. Those things just don't matter. I care how you treat me and others.

I will be drawn to you if you are oozing the self confidence that comes with knowing who you really are. That is beautiful.

Don't act ugly and then tell me you are beautiful on the inside. It doesn't work that way.

HOW YOU TREAT THE WAITER IS HOW YOU TREAT EVERYBODY

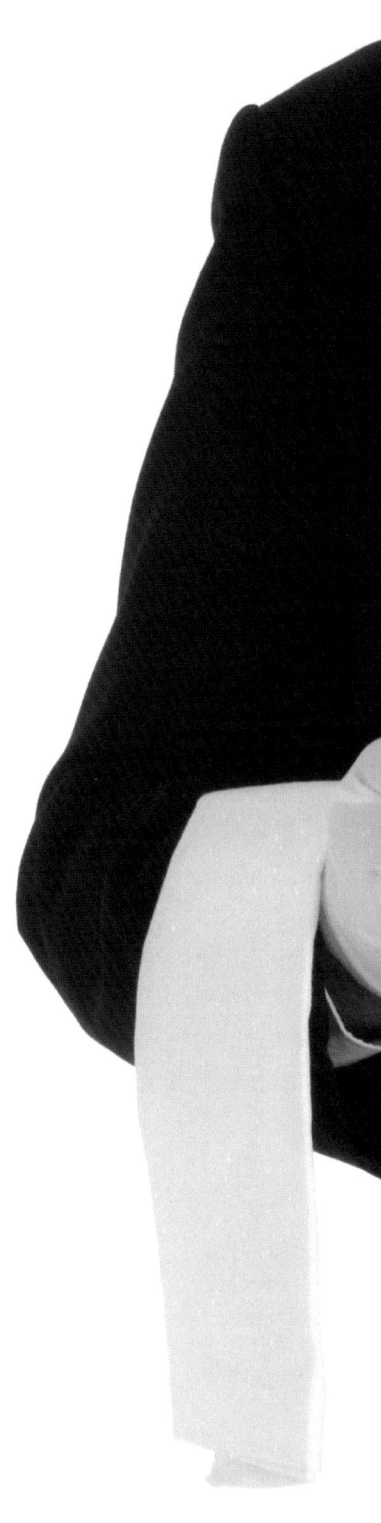

How you treat a waiter matters (and not just because he controls your food).

How you treat someone is a reflection of you, not of them. Treating a stranger well is a sign of confidence in yourself. Make those around you feel good and you will feel good.

Treat everyone like the CEO - you never know they may be someday (and sooner than you think).

WE ALL NEED
A **WINGMAN**

We could all use a little help every now and then. That is where the wingman comes in. There are a few definitions of a wingman

wing·man (wĭng'mən)
A pilot whose plane is positioned behind and outside the leader in a formation of flying aircraft.
The American Heritage® Dictionary of the English Language, Fourth Edition Copyright © 2006 by Houghton Mifflin Company.

wingman
A Wingman is a guy you bring along with you on singles outings (like to bars) that helps you out with the women.
www.urbandictionary.com

wingman
A person (male or female) who helps you out in business and social settings.
A friend or colleague who keeps your goals in mind as well as their own, creating a mutually beneficial partnership.
Aileen Bennett

Guys have known about The Wingman Effect for years. In my research for this I got to hear many funny stories about the wingmen who had 'taken one for the team'. They weren't relevant, but they were funny.

Having a wingman at a networking event, in person or online is like having your own PR agent. They can say far more flattering things about you than you can about yourself. It's much easier (and more socially acceptable) for someone else to rave about you, than you trying to tell the world how wonderful you are.

A wingman has your back, and you have hers (or his). They are your partner in networking. This partnership may last a few minutes, a whole event or be a reoccurring theme in your career.

You can have wingmen online too, they can post comments on your blog, retweet your tweets, and share your exploits and links. It's amazingly effective.

Having a wingman is like organizing the law of reciprocity. You scratch my back and I'll scratch yours. It helps everyone involved (no taking one for the team here).

If I want to meet someone at an event it is much easier for me to be introduced by someone they already know. Especially if, as they introduce you, they mention something you have in common.

You should act as a wingman, even if you don't think it will be reciprocated. It is an easy way for you to meet new people and it feels good to introduce someone else. It also makes you look confident and professional (and I am assuming that's a good thing).

If you are going to be a wingman, on or offline, please be a genuine one. If you are only about getting what you can and not helping others then you are not being a wingman - you are being small minded.

To quote Zig Ziglar
"You will get all you want in life if you help enough other people get what they want."

I NEED A BREAK (BEFORE I BREAK)

How many times have you said (to no-one in particular) that you would just love five or ten minutes peace and quiet? Just a moment to think, to pause your hectic life...

When we look for them, there are moments everywhere - In a traffic jam, in the line at the store, when you are on hold on a phone call. We miss them because we are sometimes stuck in our mindset as well as our cars.

How often do we stand in the store and examine the checkout lines? We compare one to another, count our items to see if we can sneak into the express lane, count other people's items to see if they should be there. We send our partners to stand in a different line to see if that one moves faster. We watch, we judge, we get stressed.

Why not just stand in any line, not caring if it moves fast or slow. If you are really up for a dare pick the longest line. Use the time to think, to daydream, to de-stress, to clear your mind. It's the break you've been longing for all day.

When we are stuck in traffic we need to learn to sit back and relax. Put on your favorite music and take a deep breath.

Enjoy the moments that you have longed for all day. They are everywhere. We don't have to be stressed just because we don't control when and where they happen.

*None of this applies if you have small, awake children with you. You will have to wait another few years for your break.

HERE
(if you have the right attitude)

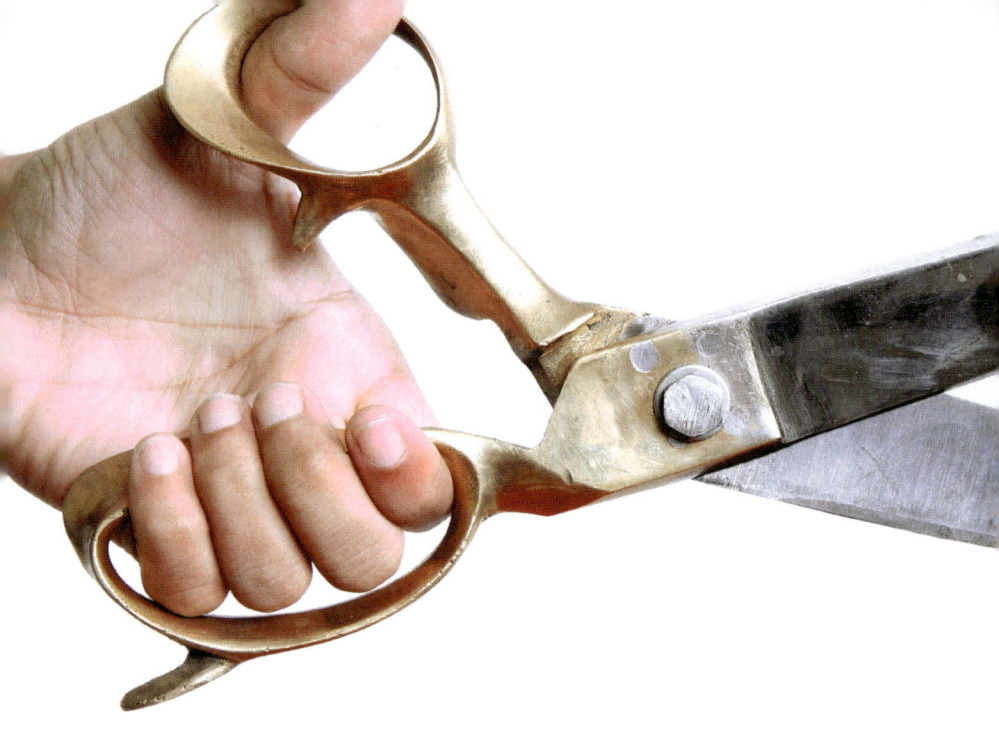

Take more risks.

We get into the habit of playing safe and playing small. It feels comfortable for a while and then we forget there is something more. We tell our children to 'be safe' and 'take care' and I sometimes think we should be telling them 'follow your instincts' and 'take a few risks'.

Its scary. You may fail. People may laugh or say "I told you so". You may feel uncomfortable. You may lose money. You may lose friends. You may lose respect. You may lose it all.

RUN WITH SCISSORS

It's scary. You may succeed. People may be jealous. You may feel uncomfortable. You may get rich. You may gain friends. You may gain respect. You may win everything.

I'm not talking about crossing the interstate wearing a blindfold here,

I'm talking about following your dreams, your instincts. Being who you suspect you were meant to be.

ASK

Go on. Start asking for what you want. You could be surprised at what happens.

Stop hoping that people will know or 'guess' what you want, however much they love you, they cannot read your thoughts.

Be careful what you ask for, you may just get it.

(If someone says no, you are no worse off than you were before, being in the same position doesn't count as a setback.)

RESPECT YOUR **COMPETITION**

Your competitors are more valuable than you realize. They drive you to be better. Great competitors can push their industry forward faster than anything else ever could.

Imagine the Olympics without athletes of equal abilities. Can you say 'snoozefest'?

Your competitors are so much more than your competition - they are potential experts in your industry, potential partners in business and charity. They are potentially your greatest allies. After all you have a lot in common.

If you have no competition, you probably have no market. Having an attitude of abundance in any market can bring you surprising results. Forming alliances can help your resources spread further, lowering costs and improving press coverage. In the right market, sharing advertising costs, marketing events, and other resources can have huge benefits to all involved.

It's about your attitude. When you meet someone in the same industry as you, you have to see the potential.

It's not just the same industry, when you meet people with the same attitude, or from the same town, or with the same target audience. Whoever you meet, wherever you meet them, they could be a great contact.

Share your ideas openly. It may seem counter-intuitive but abundance breeds more abundance. Business should benefit everyone involved.

In a tug-of-war one team may come out the winner, but no one actually gets anywhere. Imagine if you used all that effort to go in the same direction.

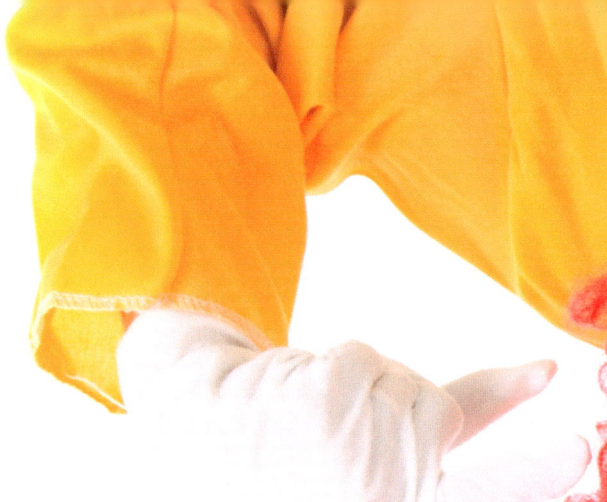

WHAT IF LIFE IS A DRESS REHEARSAL?

From an early age I was told by encouraging well-meaning people "Life isn't a dress rehearsal." I know that they meant that you only get one chance and that you should live your life like you mean it. I just prefer to think of it AS a dress rehearsal. A place where you get to try different things, play different roles. You get to make mistakes, sometimes in front of an audience, sometimes alone. A place slightly less serious than 'your only attempt to get it right'.

We get to choose our metaphors. For me, I hope life is always a dress rehearsal.

STARE AT **MODELS**

We should all spend some time every week staring at models. Role Models.

We could all use some mentors. They help us grow and develop the qualities that we see in them.

Learning from successful people is essential ingredient for your own success.

These days people are more accessible than ever, they have facebook pages, twitter accounts and all sorts of other ways to connect.

Choose role models because of particular qualities you admire. You don't have to like everything about them.

The good news is that if you like a quality in someone else, you probably already have that quality.

THIS PAGE IS A COFFEE BREAK

You deserve it

Take a moment to think about what you have read.

Take notice of the pages that stand out, those are the pages that were written for you.

If you want to know more, and join in the conversation, go to www.usingpeople.com.

You never know what you will find there!

PEOPLE I USED

My name may be on the front of the book but it wouldn't be here without a whole gang of helpers and supporters. I believe you should never miss a chance to say thank you, so here goes.

Thank you to:

My husband Sean, for putting up with me during this process, keeping the world running smoothly while I wrote and loving me still.

My family in England: Mum, Moray, Jon, Ian, Hollie, Jamie, Joe and Bennett - I miss you every moment.

Everyone who has ever believed in me and let me just be me (this matters more than you know)

Jeremy, Jesse & Cody for the belief and brains.

Gwen, for the keen eye, the sharp wit and the great photos.

Blake, for the quote page design and answering my questions.

TB, for knowing when to listen, when to tell me to suck it up.

All those who came to my studio and volunteered to have their photos taken looking silly.

The audiences that have heard this speech - your reactions led to this book.

My mastermind group, for your minds (and your hearts).

Marianne Williamson for the use of the 'our deepest fear' quote.

The Kooks, for playing the music that made me smile most while putting this together.

London, New York City, & Lafayette for being the places with the people.

Everyone who has ever asked my advice or picked my brain over coffee, lunch or a glass of wine.

CREDIT WHERE CREDIT IS DUE

Gwen Aucoin took the following photos of the following people:
p11 - Michael and Anne
p14 - Books
p19 & 20 - Abi
p22 - Annabelle
p28 - Ryan
p31 - Mary Grace
p36 - Colin
p39 - Jesse
p40 - Pinocchio
p47 - Kylie
p50 - Ryan, Kaitlin & Oliver
p65 - Brian
p66 - Sean
p78 - Hunter

The following photos are from stockphoto agencies:
p8 ©Can Stock Photo Inc./ Deanm1974, p17 ©Can Stock Photo Inc./ajt, p27 ©Can Stock Photo Inc./ wacker, p32 ©iStockphoto.com/saluha, p34 ©iStockphoto.com/acilo, p42 ©Can Stock Photo Inc./dotshock, p44 ©iStockphoto.com/Yuri_Arcurs, p49 ©iStockphoto.com/Alyssum, p52 ©iStockphoto.com/mandygodbehear, p54&55 ©Can Stock Photo Inc./ arekmalang, p58 & p97 ©Can Stock Photo Inc./hjalmeida, p60 ©Can Stock Photo Inc./ redbaron, p69 ©iStockphoto.com/rkotulan, p71 ©iStockphoto.com/IsaacLKoval, p72 ©Can Stock Photo Inc./volare2004, p77 ©iStockphoto.com/jgroup, p82 ©Can Stock Photo Inc./ italianestro, p84 ©Can Stock Photo Inc./thesupe87, p86 ©Can Stock Photo Inc./mikenorton, p88 ©Can Stock Photo Inc./paulprescott72, p90 ©iStockphoto.com/urbancow, p92 ©iStockphoto.com/morganl, p95 ©iStockphoto.com/vm, p98 ©Can Stock Photo Inc./avesun

Thank you all for your creativity.

THE NEXT PAGE **IS A GIFT**
(in more ways than one)

On the next page is one of the most powerful pieces of writing I have ever come across and one we should all at least try to live up to everyday. We hold ourselves back for all sorts of reasons and this gives us the best reason not to.
My version of this is on the flip side, it's not nearly as eloquent or beautiful but it's the same message. BE YOU, you are amazing.

This book started as a speech and developed with the help of many audiences in many cities across the globe. You can find out more (and download bonus material) at usingpeople.com.

Thanks for reading.

BE YOU

Aiken

Our deepest fear is not that we are inadequate.

Our deepest fear is that we are powerful beyond measure.

It is our light not our darkness that most frightens us.

We ask ourselves, who am I to be brilliant, gorgeous, talented and fabulous?

Actually, who are you not to be?

You are a child of God.   Your playing small does not serve the world.

There's nothing enlightened about shrinking so that other people won't feel insecure around you.

We were born to make manifest the glory of God that is within us. It's not just in some of us; it's in everyone.

And as we let our own light shine, we unconsciously give other people permission to do the same.

As we are liberated from our own fear, our presence automatically liberates others.

Marianne Williamson
(with permission) Return to Love by Marianne Williamson, Harper Collins, 1992

BE YOU
you are amazing

ABOUT THE AUTHOR

Aileen Bennett is a speaker, author and communication coach and does, whatever she does, with both cynicism and passion. Aileen moved from London, England to Lafayette, Louisiana (yes, there is a story there) where she lives with her husband Sean, and her two dogs in an alarmingly white house.

Aileen is fascinated by communication, business and beautifully designed objects. She spent the first ten years of her working life as a Graphic Designer and it shows in her approach to everything. In addition to this book, Aileen is the author of 'Notes on Shining' - a book about presentation skills, for those who don't read books on presentation skills. She also writes two weekly newspaper columns, 'That's What She Said' and 'BE YOU'.

To find out how Aileen can help you and your organization, or to discuss speaking engagements, please go to the website - thatspeaker.com, where you will always find the most up-to-date contact information. If the people in your business deal with people, then talk to Aileen.

YOU ARE ALL HEROES

CPSIA information can be obtained
at www.ICGtesting.com
226357LV00003B